TRAINING MEMOIRS
OF A
SPIRITUAL
WARRIOR
CRYSTAL SMITH
FIGHTING THE GOOD FIGHT

Training Memoirs of a Spiritual Warrior

Fighting the Good Fight

By

Crystal Smith (Author)

Vincent Smith (co- Producer)

Unless otherwise indicated, all scripture quotations are taken from the
King James Version of the Bible:

Training Memoirs of A Spiritual Warrior: Fighting the Good Fight
ISBN Copyright @2023 by Crystal Smith
ISBN (9798218337841)

Published by Crystal Smith
Lexington, South Carolina
Vincent Smith Photographer /co Producer

Table of Contents

Dedication

I dedicate this book to my Mother Margaret Crosby who has always known that I was a fighter in the natural realm. She recalls my youthful follies during my adolescent years. When I asked her about memories of my childhood, she replied in such a way that made me giggle.

I am Margaret Crosby. I am the mother of one boy Andre (Rodney) deceased; and of three girls Lisa, Cathea, and Crystal. Funny thing is, Crystal is the youngest and the most robust one. I realized it the first time I heard Crystal curse aloud. She was about two years old. I was working the graveyard shift from 1:30am to 9 in the morning. After dinner I would allow the children to play outside. To re-enter the house, they were required to come around the back. That day Crystal decided not to do this. She climbed up the steps and banged on the door and demanded that the door be opened immediately. She used the most colorful words that would even make a sailor blush. The most interesting thing concerning Crystal was that although she was the youngest of my children, she was the most spirited. As she got older she had gotten even more spirited. Until this day I am quite certain it was nothing but the Holy Spirit that had graced her.

Margaret Ann Crosby

Forward

The Bible says In Galatians 2:20 that , "Christ lives in me." In verse 3:5 it says that God has given us His Spirit. In Galatians 3:27 it says that believers are "baptized into Christ" and are "clothed" with Christ.

Crystal reminds us in her Memoir that even though we stray from God and try to do things our way, His will for our lives shall be done. His spirit is still in us. We may ignore it, or even try to run away from it, it is still there. The word tells us there is no hiding from God. (Psalm 139:8) The enemy is cunning and slick but he is no match for our true and living God. Be encouraged that the word of God is true. He will never leave nor forsake. In our weakness He is made strong. When we decide to let go and allow God to be

God is when things begin to change and happen for us. Remember the word of God says all things work together for the good them that love God and are called according to his purpose. Christ lives in us. We have His spirit. Training Memoirs of a Spiritual Warrior teaches us that we have no other choice but to be victorious. All tricks, schemes, plots, and plans of the devil are defeated so continue to fight the good fight, for we are victorious always in God.

Angie Smith

Grace's Haven, Founder

Chapter 1: BIRTHING PAINS

Jeremiah 1:4-5 Then the Word of the Lord came to me saying "Before you were born I knew; and ordained you a prophet to the nations.

I cringe to this day when I think about how my mother spoke of my feisty temperament as a child. She would tell anyone sitting around listening that "Crystal has always been very boisterous" She would even go on to say, "When I brought her home from the hospital, she would just be so angry". She would cry and scream with her fists balled up" She would go on to tell the eager listeners that she changed my diaper and fed me and still I would be fierce. Of course all the while I would be listening angrily. I hated every time she told the story. In my mind, I was like whatever! Why does she even tell it? For what purpose would it serve? As I share this stage of my life, I now know. For it was the birthing stage of the beginning of a spiritual warrior. I was born with the fight in the spirit but not yet understanding what it really was.

Although I cannot remember anything from the infant stage, I look back now and laugh. I kind of low key believed every word mother would share over and over to anyone who would listen. Believe it or not, she has told the story for over 40 years. Every time she shared it, I wanted to make her be quiet and I wanted to fight whomever, listened and agreed verbally. Sometimes I even wanted to fight her for telling it, but I knew better.

Thinking back to my elementary school years in Wilmington, Delaware, I can't say that I remember too many happy days. I can't remember really even enjoying recess. I can, however, remember that there always seemed to be some type of opposition. I felt like it was always a dooming feeling. Either I was going to have to shrink back, be quiet, or fight. It always felt like I had options other than being young and carefree. While not being able to remember my infant years so clearly, this is something that I vividly recalled throughout my adolescent years. The thing that seems really weird was, even though I was allegedly robust as an infant. There was a side of me that held great fear of the unknown. I wasn't really sure where I stood. All I remember is when the rubber met the road, I did one or two things. I commenced to fight or shrink to disappear if I could. Strangely, I was super shy and super afraid of the dark. However, when it came down to a physical fight, I stood my ground for every challenge. In Fact many times, Not only did I stand my ground, I went overboard. This went on for many years.

I carried the spirit of the fight so heavy during my adolescent years that I was referred to as crazy. Although I never started any of my altercations; everyone knew that it was a guarantee that I would retaliate. In my mind, it was always protection. I was protecting myself by any means necessary. Once I felt threatened, I could no longer control the unction to lash out.

Chapter 2: FAITH OVER FEAR

2 Timothy 1:7 - For God hath not given us the spirit of fear; but of power, and of love, and of a sound mind.

For as long as I could remember, when I was a small child there had always been a fear factor. I had always been afraid of the dark. I was afraid to speak in my classrooms when my teachers called upon me. I was afraid of what people thought of me. I was afraid for no reason. I was also afraid of things I had no reason to be afraid of. However, for as long as I can remember, I've also been boisterous, fearless, and spicy with the most ferocious temperament. The most puzzling thing was at times I maybe should have been afraid, I wasn't. That factor never dawned on me until I began to share this journey.

Instead of shutting down or taking flight from a fear or unpleasant situation, I began to fight. I lashed out at anyone and about anything I did not understand or I thought was a threat to me or invaded my personal safety place. I physically fought so much through elementary that I received paddles and even suspension at times. Through the years, every time I was confronted, my fears began to morph into something different, something more sinister. Unchecked, over the years my fears had actually manifested rage. In my mind, the fight worked. It kept people from bullying me. It made people fear me instead.   As I grew in age and matured in spirit, I realized that the physical retaliation of fighting no longer worked for me the way I wanted it to. It eventually began to work against me. Something had to give.

Regrettably, I found myself hindered by my own tendencies. The inherent need for an unyielding determination in the face of challenges was within me, yet I clung to it fiercely. It became perplexing how a trait meant to shield me could morph into a force capable of self-destruction. The coherence of my actions began to unravel, and the logic behind my instinct to engage in battles, disputes, or misconceptions seemed increasingly elusive. Despite understanding the imperative to cease fighting in various situations, I remained unwilling to relinquish my own prescribed methods of self-protection, trapped in a paradox of my own creation.

The conflict within me intensified as the realization dawned that what once served as my shield had transformed into a potential weapon against myself. Each instance of opposition or misunderstanding became a battlefield where I struggled to reconcile the necessity of surrendering my instinctive need to fight. It was a revelation that left me grappling with the contradicting nature of self-preservation turning into self-sabotage. The clarity I sought eluded me, and in the midst of this internal struggle, nothing seemed to make sense anymore. This feeling left me at a crossroad between holding onto my fierce determination and embracing the vulnerability required to navigate through life and realize everyone wasn't an enemy.

Chapter 3: THE AWAKENING

"The kingdom of God is within you." - Luke 17:21

As I entered middle school, I began to realize the power of presentation and the power that lived inside of me. I learned that the divine presence and spiritual awakening are found within oneself. I began to look inward for my connection to my gifts for my strength. As I performed with the girl scouts, or played the trumpet, or played sports, I felt a surge of confidence. However, I still was not speaking in front of groups. I literally got goose bumps and a great spirit of nervousness when the opportunity presented itself. This season of my life was especially difficult. The middle school years presented challenges that could have hindered my progress if I wasn't so determined in everything I attempted to accomplish. I was socially awkward. I didn't have fancy expensive clothes. I wasn't part of the in-crowd and nor did I desire to be. I marched to the beat of a different drummer. I never cared to be too much like other people. I felt that it was too constricting to my free spirit. I had a different way of doing things.

Unfortunately, it usually got me in trouble. However, during these middle school years the Lord graced me a little more courage to at least indulge in my creative gifts. Being a member of the girl scout troop at Tabernacle Baptist Church in Wilmington, Delaware provided a safe haven for my creative gifts. While participating as part of the girl scouts, I was able to sell girl scout cookies, do community service, and participate in the drill team. The drill team became one of my favorite pastimes. With each parade we marched in, I gained a little more confidence each time. Being dressed in my brownie suit with our matching saddle shoes made me feel a little like I was on the come up. My sister Cathea and our best friends Dianne and Bernice were on the drill team. We did everything together. The Wilmington Scouts was what we will call ourselves as we chanted and marched through the downtown streets of the eastside right past the famous four squares. There were hundreds of supporters and they would yell and cheer us on. I'm grateful for that experience because I know it was one of the activities that helped build some of my presentation skills.

I wasn't a very good singer so I know being in the choir wasn't one of the activities that built my voice. If I were to be honest, I believe it was one of the reasons that almost helped to shrink my voice. As I mentioned I was sort of a loner who kind of did my own thing and usually my own thing led to a bit of trouble. Well one day in choir rehearsal I felt the need to write how I felt on the back of a fan. I felt like Ms. K. treated me differently because I wasn't one of the popular or fancy dressed well to do children. I felt every facial expression and misdeed she extended to me. Well I took it upon myself to write on the fan during choir rehearsal. "I hate Ms. K". Yes, I honestly felt like that. I wish I could have fought her. Yes, I was a bit low key passive aggressive. The only problem was that she was about maybe a couple of years my senior.

Unfortunately, Ms. K found the fan and unfortunately, whomever was sitting next to me ratted me out. That day Ms. K no longer allowed me to sing in the choir. The crazy thing is that no one even came to my defense. That day, I wrote Ms. K off forever. It was just as well because soon after that, I would never have to deal with her ever again.

One morning we got up to go to church as usual and I distinctly remember mom not taking the turn to go in the direction of the church. All five children immediately looked at each other in silence. We dared not to say anything because, well let's just say, we dared not say anything. There were five children and until this day, I don't know how but every Sunday All five children plus mom piled into the Chevrolet and made our way to worship. This particular Sunday we all rode in silence and anticipation as we looked wide eyed as mom drove into New Castle, Delaware. It was a bit of a ride from our usual Sunday morning destination. The car finally came to our destination. We remained quiet and no one said a Word. As mom put the car in park, she gave directions for us to unload. To this day I never asked the other children what was in their minds. I thought to myself, Oh, we're visiting a new church. Okay, I can deal with this. The new church was actually in a school. It was a new start-up church. I felt comfortable walking in. I wondered if they would like us. I know that sounds crazy concerning a church.

Unfortunately, I definitely didn't feel liked or loved by the other church. Upon entering the building we were greeted as I had never experienced before. This was a church of diversity. There were many different races. When we walked in I remember some of the members putting their arms out to greet us. They told us that they were really glad to see us and that we were welcome. This was awesome and intriguing. Tabernacle had never greeted us in that fashion. I always felt as if they were irritated by us at times. Call it what you may but a child has a discernment as well. It may not always be as mature as an adult's but, they can feel hate and animosity too. Well the feeling that I experienced upon entering this church was enlightening. I remember being nervous. However, the greeters had definitely been trained in their job. It definitely was a natural gift for them. They were in the right place at the right time. I had never felt so welcome in my life. Victory Christian Fellowship Outreach became our new church home. Pastor Gary and Faye Whetstone became our new Pastor and First lady. This would be my last time changing churches until I moved to South Carolina after graduating from college.

At Victory, I can honestly say, I got victory over a few more roadblocks the enemy tried to present. At Victory, I interacted with youth my age. It didn't matter if I didn't have name brand clothes or my hair wasn't long and straight. They accepted me for me. I began to learn the true love of Christ. I began to learn beyond simple Bible stories. It was a new beginning.

I remember one Sunday the choir was singing as beautifully as they always did. I was really feeling it. The spirit was high. I just feel the excitement. The choir had a full band. I remember after the song ended a member stood up and spoke in unknown tongues. Well I sort of heard it before but really didn't understand it. I watched attentively. Of course no one knew what the individual was saying, but they did not interrupt her.

When she finished she sat down. There was a brief pause. Then someone in the band stood up, put down their stringed instrument and declared the Words of the Lord. I was a young adolescent but I knew beyond a shadow of a doubt that what had just happened was the manifestation of the Holy Spirit. I was in awe. I couldn't stop thinking about how awesome that was. I knew God was real but this encounter was so surreal that it would forever be etched in my memory. It opened a curiosity to the miracles of God. I actually began to enjoy going to youth groups and Sunday School. I no longer dreaded going to the house of the Lord.

Victory Christian Fellowship was a place I could thrive. It was a place I experienced miracles first hand. When I was around 8 years old, my family noticed a lump on my neck. Being unsure of what it was, they didn't allow me to play freely or jump on the trampoline one summer when we were visiting our cousins in South Carolina. I didn't notice anything wrong with my throat and I didn't feel anything different either.

Well once we got back home to Delaware my mom made an appointment with the family doctor. The doctor agreed that the growth was abnormal. It was diagnosed as a cyst. I ended up having to have surgery to cut it out. This eventually left me with stitches under my neck. The peers at my school were super cruel. They would sometimes refer to me as scar face and made assumptions that I may have tried to commit suicide due to the cut under my neck. This period sent me back into a seclusive type of behavior. I always kept my head down in fear of someone seeing my stitches and wondering if I was suicidal or not. I began to hold in my resentment and anger from the teasing and bullying.

At times when I least expected, it would all come rushing out and I would respond with fighting or cursing at anyone or any particular thing that triggered me. I remember punching the playground safety monitor in the nose because he told me I couldn't go from one side of the playground to the other. The principal paddled me respectfully. There was another time I remember my brother turning the lights off in the basement and screaming that the boogie man was going to get me. I cursed every word aloud that I knew how to as I ran up the stairs from the dark basement. I remember wanting to beat the living snot out of him but he was bigger than me so I just said the best rendition of grown up curse words I could share with him. It felt pretty good too I recall. Unfortunately, once the basement door opened my mother was on the other side. She welcomed me out of the dark basement for a swift whipping.

On another occasion my brother locked me outside in the backyard. We had a dog but I was kind of scared of it a little. Well my brother told me the dog was going to get me and he ran in the kitchen from the backyard and locked the door. I banged on the door and commenced cursing once again. It wasn't too long ago that I had gotten a whipping for cursing and demanding my brother let me out of the basement. What did I do? I became a repeat offender. However, not only did I curse and threaten my brother to open the backdoor, I banged and banged on the window. Well before you know it, I crashed the glass with my fist. I was so furiously angry with him, I did not even realize that I had gashed my forearm. I ended up having to get stitches.

Regrettably", there was no sympathy for the incident. After returning home from the hospital and having to get stitches, I got a whipping for crashing the window. I was angry at the world. I was angry at the world. In my mind, I wish I could have grabbed mom and told her to stop whipping me because she had no idea how afraid I was. Moreover, I wanted to beat up my brother up at the same time. I was furious that he frightened me so bad on purpose. I knew I couldn't because I was the youngest and the smallest thing in the house. This is how my temperament was. It was outta control at nine years old. The thoughts and retaliation in mind was off the charts.

Fast forward, back to our new church we were attending. Victory wasn't just teaching us Bible stories, I really learned more about the true and living God. Not only did I learn about the Power of God, I got firsthand experience. It had been about a year since my scar healed from the removal of the cyst when my mother noticed it was growing back. We ended up having a second surgery to remove it again. The second surgery wasn't finished healing thoroughly when they noticed that the cyst was growing back a third time. I couldn't understand why this was happening. On top of being shy, I had to endure this again. During the teasing and bullying, I really couldn't talk or say anything because the doctors wanted me to refrain from using muscles in my throat if that made any sense. Well one Sunday morning my mother got me out of the children's church and brought me up to the altar for prayer. I remember Pastor Gary Whetstone praying over my throat and I remember my mother crying and then we went back to our seats. I didn't think too much more about it throughout the remainder of the service.

That afternoon we had to ride to Maryland to pick up my sister Cathea from Chesapeake-Campgrounds. It was just my mother and I as we took the one hour drive. I remember the drive up clearly. It was a beautiful day outside and the sun beamed so brightly into our white Chevrolet. I fell asleep on the drive. I awoke to my mother shouting my name. At first I awoke saying to myself, "what did I do now?" "This woman is always hollering!" My goodness! I was asleep, I couldn't have done anything". It took me a little while to get myself together. I actually had to come out of the sleep. I vividly remember. It was as if God had put me into a deep slumber. Mom called my name a few times and I didn't answer even though I was right next to her. Because I didn't wake right away she raised her voice in a panic. I believe she thought I passed away on the drive. When I sat up, I felt something wet on my neck. The cyst had burst on its own and it never grew back again. That was over forty-five years ago. Although I was a young busy child, I knew that a miracle had just taken place. As Psalms 119:11 says, I hid that miracle in my heart. Unfortunately, I still continued to sin against God. While I was intrigued concerning the miracles of God, it did not stop all of my disobedience. I still dealt with the fear factor. As odd as it seemed, the fear issue would come and go. I never knew when it was going to manifest. I use the word manifest because apparently I was not in fear all the time. This baffled me, especially since I was in my middle school years. Fear gripped me so strongly at times that I was afraid to get out of bed in the middle of the night to use the bathroom. I would hold steadfast and fall asleep. Sadly, due to my not getting up to use the restroom, I would wet the bed once I fell back sleep. This even carried over into middle school. The thing that baffled my family was that, within the same 24 hours I'd be fighting someone around the neighborhood. It would most of the time be someone older or bigger than myself. I remember one day my eldest sister was having a bit of trouble with someone that lived in the neighborhood when she was staying. I intentionally walked 12 blocks towards the eastside to pay her a visit. I put a knife in my jacket pocket. In my mind I was going to set the record straight or scare her to pieces. I didn't have a solid plan but I knew I was going to make a statement. My sister ended up fighting the girl and I ran up and pulled out a huge knife out of my jacket. Not only did I scare the girl fighting my sister, I scared my sister as well. They both screamed at the same time. The girl ran down the street and my sister Lisa's eyes got huge as golf balls. I looked at her to assure her that I was just coming to protect her. All I can remember was her saying, "Noooooo Nooooo", you can't do that Crystal.

At those times the fear seemed non-existent, whether it was fighting or the aftermath of the manner in which I fought. My siblings would refer to me as the wild child. I can't say that it was a title that I didn't work hard at. It seemed as though at times I lived a double life. I would fearfully get through the evening and wildly fumble through the days. Strangely, No matter how much trouble I got into, I was covered. God always gave me a way out. There were plenty of times I had lost my temper during a misunderstanding. Many times my temperament led me to altercations. I was so relieved once I graduated from middle school. Although I didn't leave behind my ferocious temperament, the bullying did slack up. For that I was grateful.

High School was a bit easier to mesh with my peers. I made the cheering squad as a freshman. Those years at Glasgow High School in Newark, Delaware were somewhat sweet memories. As I cheered for football, played basketball, (which I was horrible at) and ran track I was able to build up a bit of self-confidence. I was performing in the midst of large crowds again. I was not yet speaking on a whim in front of groups on my own. The fear fact would still grip me at times. I remember that the great fear that I experienced at night had slacked up some. I would walk the city streets at night by myself and without an ounce of fear. I would walk from the West Side to the East Side at times. As far as being afraid of sleeping at night, I never really had to be alone and it seemed as though someone was always home at night in a house with five children.

Now that I had become a little more sociable, I was able to step out of my comfort zone a tad bit more. I was always very creative and it turns out that I was a bit dramatic as well. This characteristic went very well with my interest in public speaking. The crazy thing is that I was still afraid of the crowd. However, I could speak very well from the reviews of my camp counselor from the Old Asbury Church in Wilmington and my 9th grade English teacher Mrs. Lightjames. I had managed to pick up a technique of focusing on an object in the rear of the room. I had mastered that technique and nailed it every time.

While I was crafting my gifts, the enemy still ran rampant concerning my temperament.

I could perform boldly and with exuberance along with a team or in a group but using my voice only to speak up for myself or ask a question in class was a task that sent unshakeable fear to my whole being. As I look back, sometimes all it required was for me to open my mouth. Instead, I continued to shrink down and if I was met with opposition, usually a fight was on the horizon. I had operated in this manner so long that the school put me on contract. I was sent to the school board. The contract stipulated that I would be prohibited from engaging into any more altercations for the remainder of the year. If I had violated the contract, I would be suspended from the entire school district. My mom had gone to the meetings to fight for me. I was just reacting to all my insecurities by fighting everyone else.

I believe at this point, that the district was tired of my mother and myself. The school district offered me no other alternative. I would have to cease and desist with all the fighting. This forced me to approach situations differently.

Because I had no other choice but to straighten up, I did. I got through the remainder of high school without any more serious altercations.

I believe to this day, the contract really helped. I should say it helped temporarily.

In this same period of my life I remember the movie Freddy Kruger coming out. I'm almost certain that that movie reopened some doors in my life that I thought I was beyond. It is still so etched in my mind because I remember thinking to myself, what if my classmates knew that I was afraid of the dark? I went right back to sleeping with the lights on. I never slept with my arm hanging over the bed. I had the fear that a long arm would come from under the bed and grab me. I would beat myself up for even watching some of the movie because before I watched it, I had begun to grow. Once I watched it, the spirit of fear began to take hold of my carefree being. I noticed my behavior became slightly unbalanced once again. What would people think if they knew of my fear of the dark? How much more awkwardly would they treat me if they knew I had so many secret fears? Between the time of opening another door of fear from watching the movie and the coming to an end of summer time; a new adventure was awaiting me. High School was on the horizon.

During my high school years, fear was a constant presence in my life. Little did I know that fear could trigger a multitude of emotions, including anger. As a freshman, I surprisingly made it onto the cheer squad, and that set the tone for my entire high school experience. I was a natural at connecting with people. I was the life of the crowd many times. It didn't matter who you were, I could relate to you. I had a laid-back personality, but I didn't tolerate any nonsense.

Luckily, I didn't associate myself with the kind of crowd that would purposely provoke me. Throughout my four years at Glasgow High School, I can vividly recall three instances where fear overwhelmed me, triggering a range of unknown emotions. The first of these occurred during my freshman year when the state had just integrated schools. We were bused 30 minutes away from our neighborhood, and tensions were running high.

On our way home, as our bus was heading back to our neighborhood, a group of hostile students ran alongside the bus, hurling racial slurs at us. In retaliation, we began shouting back. Suddenly, bricks were thrown through the bus window, shattering the glass into pieces. The bus driver slammed on the brakes, causing chaos and panic among the students. Some were covered in glass, and tears began to stream. I watched in horror, unable to comprehend what was happening. We had been attacked, and I felt powerless because I couldn't fight back. It was a feeling of vulnerability that I had never experienced before, and I despised it. How could this happen? Was this what the next four years of busing would be like?

As a young freshman in high school, this incident opened the floodgates of fear within me. I had always felt invincible, but now, that illusion was shattered. However, the responsible students were eventually identified, and the attacks ceased. The bus rides back to our neighborhood became long but safe, and I could finally breathe a sigh of relief. Although fear remained a constant companion throughout my high school years, that initial incident taught me the importance of resilience and the strength to overcome adversity. It was a lesson that would shape my character and drive me to stand up against injustice. Despite the fear, I refused to let it define me and continued to navigate my high school journey with determination and a newfound understanding of the power of emotions.

On another occasion where I felt fear was with this girl named Shantel. For some reason she would always taunt me. We weren't even from the same side of town. My family lived on the West side of town in Wilmington and Shantel and her family lived on the lower East side of Wilmington, Delaware. She even rode a different bus. We were not in any classes together either. I don't even know how she even came to target me. In any event, I became her target. My heart would literally flutter once I'd seen her coming my way. She was very buff and taller in stature than myself. I was necessarily afraid to get into the actual tangle. I was more afraid of unleashing the anger that I had worked so hard to contain over the years. I was afraid of the crazy. I say crazy because each time, I lost it and let the emotions roll, people ended up referring to me as crazy. I laugh to myself as I think back because I actually did act out in a crazy manner.

This one particular day, I made up my mind that I was tired of her taunting. There was a word in my mind. I was to stand up to her and tell her that she did not phase me anymore. It was a notion so strong, and I made up my mind that it was going to happen. I was going to tell her the next time she sought to intimidate and bully me. Well the day came. I was walking down the hall. She was getting closer. I saw that she stepped over to get in my path. For what I didn't even know. She was like the aggravating jolly green giant. Today I wasn't shrinking down or being quiet. Once she got closer, I belted out loud. "You don't phase me!" I don't know if she was taken aback because she didn't understand the word, or she was surprised that I stood up to her. She seemed stunned and seemed to mumble. To this day, I couldn't believe it but it worked. People couldn't believe that I stood up to her, students began to surround us and shout ohhhhhhh ohhhhhh! A crowd swarmed around us so quickly and teachers came and that was that. From that point on, I knew she would not attempt to bully me again. Surprisingly, she didn't either. The strangest thing is that about one month after the incident, we had to make a hospital visit. We had to visit my father's uncle. His name was uncle Sam.

It turns out that he was doing so well. It was important for us to go see him. I was kind of uneasy about going into the room. I really liked uncle Sam. I felt that spirit of fear coming over me. This time it was fear of the uncertainty of Uncle Sam. Upon coming out of the room, there was another group, another family that was there to see him. I stood in total confusion as I saw Shantel. Could it be? Was this girl related to me? Oh my goodness! She was. Turns out that she herself had been battling some emotional roller coasters that made her bully other people. That was the information that the guidance counselor briefly explained to my mother. That is how I became one of her targets. That day I looked in Shantel's eyes as she walked into that hospital room and I saw fear in her eyes. We both gave one another a half, gentle, easy smile. Neither of us spoke a word of that day for the remainder of our high school tenure.

As time progressed on, my math class stepped up a notch to Algebra. I was never that good at math. Stepping up to algebra sucked. I hated math. I couldn't understand it. I didn't want to understand it. I cut classes to avoid it. I stopped cutting class once I realized that I needed it to graduate. I remember sitting in the back of the class one day crying. Tears were rolling down my cheeks. I needed God to help me if I was ever going to understand Algebra and graduate. I cried in silence the entire class. The crazy thing is, the teacher or no one even asked what was wrong. I literally cried and pondered the entire class. I prayed silently to God to please help me with math. I can't even recall the day nor the hour. However, a light came on one day. I slowed down and I caught the basics of algebra and I made it out of high school with a C. I know it was nobody but God. Today I will not even do any kind of sales job or money counting job. I literally do not enjoy it at all.

I remember during the season of struggling with math, I would enjoy nothing more but to exert my strength and energy into sports after school. It was a complete relief to me. Athletics and physical activities were my strong point and where I thrived in my true potential as an athlete. Senior year brought a newfound confidence and determination within me. I had honed my skills in cheerleading, basketball, and track, and I was ready to showcase my abilities.

Cheerleading was a passion. The thrill of performing complex stunts and captivating the crowd with synchronized routines filled me with immense joy. I was a key member of the squad, trusted with executing difficult maneuvers and bringing energy to every game. The camaraderie among my teammates made the experience even more fulfilling, as we pushed each other to reach new heights.

In basketball, despite not being the most skilled player on the court, I discovered my niche on the defensive end. With lightning-fast reflexes and a relentless drive, I became a force to be reckoned with. I relished in shutting down opponents, stealing the ball, and making crucial defensive plays that turned the tide in our favor. It was in those moments that I truly felt like a warrior, defending my team's honor.

Track was where my natural athleticism truly shone. I excelled in sprinting events, effortlessly gliding across the track with every stride. The rush of adrenaline as I crossed the finish line, pushing my body to its limits, was addicting. I embraced the discipline and dedication required to be a successful track athlete, constantly striving to improve my speed and technique.

As senior year progressed, I realized that my love for athletics extended beyond the physical aspect. It was about pushing myself mentally and emotionally, discovering my strengths and weaknesses, and learning the importance of teamwork and resilience. Athletics had become my warrior training, preparing me for the challenges that life would throw my way.

With each game, competition, and practice, I grew more confident in my abilities. Senior year became a turning point in my life, as I began to see the potential within myself. I realized that my passion for athletics had shaped me into a determined and resilient individual.

Looking back, I am grateful for the opportunities I had to participate in athletics and physical activities.

They kept me in shape, taught me valuable life lessons, and allowed me to embrace my inner warrior. Senior year was a time of self-discovery and growth, and I was proud of the person I had become through my love for sports. Life was progressing well.

I was a senior on the varsity cheer squad for football. I played basketball the best I could and I came back from an injury and completed my senior year of track successfully. I lettered in track and cheerleading. Finishing my senior year gave me a boost of confidence that would carry me into my freshman year of college. While preparing for my first year in college, I secured a job at the baseball field. It was great money and a great work environment. Unfortunately, I let my guard down, concerning my temperament. I can't even remember what the disagreement was about. However, the old man called anger had unexpectedly risen before I knew it.   While working during the summer at the baseball field I got into a disagreement with another co-worker and lost that job. Luckily school was starting.   It was time for a fresh start where no one knew me.   Maybe I could start over and control this anger thing.

Chapter 4: THE PRESSING

John 16:33 Rest assured, this life is filled with pressure, difficulty, trial, and loss. Jesus said "in the world you will have tribulation but take heart, I have overcome the world'

I made it to college. I was a freshman at Morris College in Sumter, South Carolina. Things were going pretty well for me. I made the cheering squad as a freshman and became the captain. I was voted as Miss Freshman as well. I pledged A Sweet social club under my eldest brother Roddney who happened to be in his senior year. I can say my first year went ok. My second year, I was voted Miss Cheerleader. My popularity and social skills began to shape up. Unfortunately, with popularity comes obstacles. The bullies began to come out of the woodworks. I had not yet conquered my temperament. The contract from the high school just halted it briefly. I had gotten into a few altercations. I was able to bypass getting in trouble. Unfortunately, the final altercation I had gotten into during my sophomore year at the college took a toll on my progress. I ended up getting expelled from the college. I felt a huge blow from my actions. As I think back, I probably still would have made the same decision to protect myself physically. It was all I had ever resorted to as a form of coping. I had always bottled my feelings up until they exploded like a tsunami. This particular day I was approached by two bullies and I refused to be the bigger person. I lashed out at both of them and threatened to slash both of them with whatever I could get my hands on. Unfortunately, at the time the school was on accreditation review. They were on edge about being viewed as a school with violence. They made the decision that changed the way I felt about the entire world. A decision had to be made. I had been expelled. It seemed as though the world stopped. This opened the door for depression and resentment towards myself.   I constantly beat myself up emotionally.   I left the school and went to live with my brother Andre for a few months. During those months I took some time to reflect. I worked at my brother Andre and his wife Ladawn's only black owned movie theater in Durham, North Carolina. I also took a part time job at Wendy's. In spare days when I was off, my brother taught me how to drive a stick shift. I felt the cloud of failure lift from me a bit. It felt like I was making some progress in life.

When a new season began for school, I enrolled at Allen University. God had allowed me to have a fresh start. This school year showed great promise. I joined the cheering squad once again and cheered all four years. I can honestly say I avoided any serious altercations throughout my four year stay at the college.   I also engaged a bit deeper into public speaking. I joined the speech team under Dr. Mills and together with my team we won several awards competing on a national level. Little did I realize that that preparation would play a part in the plans God had prepared in advance.   I did have a few misunderstandings. However, they never led to full blown altercations. However, my lively personality sometimes kept me in trouble with the dorm mothers and sometimes my instructors. While away in college I had strayed away from attending church. I still believed in the Word of God and I always voiced that I loved God. Sheepishly, I just wasn't moved enough to visit the house of God while I was away at college. Chapel was still required once a week for every student since it was an AME school supported largely by the AME church. Without a firm hand to guide and encourage me to engage in Christian fellowship or the house of the Lord once a week; it never happened. Sadly, it didn't bother me either that I wasn't prompted to worship. As far as I was concerned, I had been in church my entire life. I wasn't going spend two days out of the week sitting still listening to the same ole' information week in and week out. I laugh to myself as I recount this. It sounds sinful by some Christian's standards but I was just enjoying my youth. Fortunately, God's blessings rained on the just as well as the unjust. I was finally experiencing freedom and fun or so I thought. It seemed as though the season of fighting was behind me. I was now getting into the mischievous things. I was cutting class, drinking during the week and on the weekends, clubbing when I could, and sneaking out past curfew. One time we had a flat tire and we even stole a tire off of another car so we could make it to the famous Club

Fountain Blue. I was enjoying living on the edge. Coming near to the end of my senior year, I found out I needed an additional physical education class in order to graduate. I remember praying so fervently for God to make a way so I could graduate on time. I prayed morning, noon, and night. The Lord provided as He had done so many times before. I was able to pay around $200 for a physical education class at Benedict College which was across the street from Allen University. Amazingly, the physical education class offered was dance 101 under the late Harold Odom. The way God showed out with this one was just plain amazing. Everything lined up perfectly. I just happened to be in a leg brace. An old basketball injury had recently resurfaced. However it was in the healing stage so I was able to finish the class successfully. After that quarter finished, my older Sister Cathea along with Alumni Sorors succeeded in bringing the AKA's back to the school yard of Allen University. She invited me to join the illustrious Sisterhood of Alpha Kappa Alpha. I looked up to her in a sense of being a more sophisticated young lady. She was more mature during times when I would flip my lid. I accepted the offer to join the sorority. I passed the interview process and received an acceptance letter. I thought to myself, God has to be looking out for me because in my mind, I was nowhere near sophisticated. I felt cute sometimes and maybe sexy at times, but never sophisticated. As I look back, I now realize that the enemy had my image of myself twisted with his lies as well. For Psalms 139:13-14 declares that I had been fearfully and wonderfully made. It took a lot of grooming for my sister to get me to the final day of crossing. I laugh now as I think back to her warning before we ventured in. In her exact words, "Now you can't be acting all crazy and stuff like you do. You have to calm down. They don't go for that stuff."

Maybe it was because of her warning, or maybe because she spoke to that busy little girl inside me. In any event I got through the entire process successfully. Humorously, deep down inside, I was saying, "wow" look at me! Crystal Smith. I am actually a member of the illustrious Alpha Kappa Alpha Sorority. Becoming a member had thrusted me into a new level of social life. I enjoyed every minute. I didn't pledge until my senior year in college. It was also my final semester before I graduated. I felt it was a cool way to end the school year.

After graduating from college I started working in the clubs. I was waitressing and working the front door. I landed a job in a recording studio. A well-known gambler and hustler became my boss. He went by the nickname of Spike. He would invite my sister and I, and all of our friends to all of his social get-togethers. I was pretty well etched into the club scene. I had begun clubbing Monday night at the Fountain Blue, Wednesday nights at club Secret Thursday Nights back at the Fountain Blue and some Saturdays at the Purple Rain or the Night Owl. We pretty much had a schedule. Clubbing and drinking in the middle of the week became a regular for me. However, I began to get sloppy with it. I got into work one Monday and my boss informed me that one of the security guards at the Fountain Blue informed him that he needed to check his secretary because she was a little drunk and her mouth was offensive. He told my boss that he would have taken me into custody if I wasn't Spike's secretary. I knew God was looking out for me again. I say that because, the way my bank account was set up then, it couldn't accommodate bail money. I was fresh out of college still partying.

It was almost a full year after graduation and I still hadn't found my footing in life. I was just going along with the flow. I had so many talents and yet I still felt almost useless in making my mark in society as a successful grad. Nonetheless, I continued to party and club weekend after weekend. My sister and I were rooming together at this time. We had found a quaint little apartment in the Columbia area. One day we received a call that would change the dynamics of all five children. Our eldest brother Rodney had passed. I immediately thought of our last conversation. He was reminding me who I really was. He was down in Columbia from Kentucky for my sister's and I college graduation. I asked if I could use his car to go visit some associates. I refer to them as associates because I knew they were not my friends. They didn't care about me and I knew it. Obviously, my brother knew it as well. Strangely enough, I still longed to be in their presence, as if it would make me cooler. When I look back now, I know I had not known half of the power and plans the father had in store for me. I was literally spending time with peers who awoke around 10am in the morning only to light up a blunt, make club plans for the evening, and or plot out their next drug deal. It never dawned on me that in one moment all that I worked for could be taken in one traffic stop. Even in that season God continued to cover me in my naive state of mind. One day I was watching television and a special news alert came over the screen. There had been a large drug bust in the Midlands. The video panned across a long table of drugs, money, and weapons. I heard the name of one associate in particular. I then saw the plastic bags, what they called dime bags on the street. I had gotten those bags for my associate from a store called "If It's Paper" Only thing, the bags were filled with marijuana. I couldn't believe my eyes. I was in their company just a few days prior. God did it again. In spite of my plans, He still permitted His plans to go forth. I look at it as if God Himself intervened. He will end a relationship if in fact the enemy intends to use the relationship to end you. I am so glad the Lord loved me and still loves me more than I loved myself at that time. Although in disbelief that my associate had made prime time news, I was more relieved that I was nowhere around when it went down. In the following months, I continued to work at the recording studio, frequent the club, and party as usual.

I soon met a gentleman named Scottie at the Club Night Owl. He would change my life forever. My sister, my friends and myself were all standing to the right of the bar and I saw a young man with his head bent down. I wondered why anyone would be in a club with their head down.

I told my friends to watch as I bumped him on the head with my hips. I was going to get his attention. I wasn't looking for a man. I was just being ornery. He looked up at me the first time I bumped him and assumed it was an accident and put his head back down. I was determined just to harass him for no reason. My confidence was off the chart that evening. My friend Stephanie knew him. She told me that he was a really good guy. She stressed that out of all his friends he had a really good heart and was genuine. Well that was all I needed to hear. I dared to bump him again, and I did. He put his head up and this time we spoke. I laughed and told him I was just playing and we both laughed. The music was on point and I wanted another drink. I excused myself and went to the bar. As I was ordering my drink, the gentleman came over to ask me to dance. I agreed to go on the dance floor. He really wasn't a great dancer in my eyes, but I got a good vibe from him. It was time to leave because the club was closing. As we left the club, I took a piece of perfumed note paper with my number on it to him. I told him to smell the paper and think of me when he got home. I believe he followed directions because I got a call. Until this day, he tells a different story, but I have receipts. We always laugh at this now.

I know God sent Vincent Prescott Smith to be my husband. I was not looking for a steady boyfriend or husband for that matter. I was just being free and spontaneous living my best broken life partying from club to club with a college degree. Vincent went by the name Scottie because he claimed neither his first nor middle name did not represent the lifestyle he was living at the time. We laugh now as we remember how he behaved. It was like something of a thug. There were no tough guys walking the streets with a name such as Vincent

Prescott. Even though I heard all the stories of club fights, street fights, and one really bad knife fight that nearly ended his life, I knew I had a gem. I hid it in my heart.   Vincent and myself found ourselves having our first love child. We named her Alecia'. She was and still is a beautiful and vivacious soul. We tied the knot a year later. Alecia' would be one of the reasons given to Scottie and myself to straighten up and leave the streets and club scene. Three years passed and we had our son Vincent. We both doubled down and focused on our new family.

Life was good and we were moving along. I had less temperament outbreaks and Scottie pressed more within the church.

Unfortunately, motherhood and marriage presented uncharted territory for me. At times of frustration, I resorted back to anger and lashing out. What would I do if I failed? How was I going to make it as a good mother? My uncertainties and fear of not measuring up went on for a large portion of the beginning years of our marriage. The fear continuously had me in flight mode. I would always leave or shut down. As I grew a little older, I changed my response. Instead of shutting down or taking flight from a fear or unpleasant situation, I began to fight. I lashed out at anyone and about anything I did not understand or I thought was a threat to me. We began to spend more time within the activities of the church.

As I matured in spirit, I realized the physical retaliation of fighting no longer worked for me. It began to work against me. It was costing me relationships, jobs, and a sincere connection with my husband and children. After I had enough of the enemy beating up on me, keeping me in bondage, and holding me back from the mandate placed on my life.   I asked the Father one question that would change my whole life. I asked God. Can He show me great things? There had to be better reasons than just existing, going to work, going to church, and home. I wanted to experience the miracles, and the God that people sang and shouted about. I knew there had to be more to life than what I was living. That day I know God heard my plea. Over the next few years, I began to study warfare. I used the bold fight I had inside of me to battle for the Lord. It was a tedious journey. I made many mistakes and was often misunderstood. My strong passion to protect God's people was often mistaken for anger. I changed my circle and began to study more on my own. I changed the company I kept, and began to settle in God's will. When I was single I used to dance in the clubs all night long. I still enjoyed dancing but in this season I changed my dancing audience. I soon began to praise dance for the Lord and teach other young people to worship through dance.

As the children grew in age, I was forced to grow more in the ways of the Lord. I began to actually intently live out the scripture 1 Corinthians 13:11, "When I was a child, I spoke as a child, I understood as a child, I thought as a child: but when I became a man, I put away childish things". In my case, not a man, but a Woman of God who would be one who would war for God and for the people of God.

Chapter 5: RELATIONSHIP VS RELIGION IS WEAPON AND WARFARE

John 14:6 "Jesus answered, 'I am the way and the truth and the life. No one comes to the Father except through me.'"

Scottie came out of the street, but got closer to religion. Until this day I say, I felt he got closer to religion and not God because our relationship began to get rocky. I knew that a relationship with God was supposed to help strengthen your relationship with your soulmate. However, that was not the case for my husband and I. Not only did we begin to grow more apart, unfortunately, I actually began to resent him. I would look in disgust as he fellowshipped and maneuvered his way around other Christians. He had so much patience with them. However, I felt like I was walking on eggshells around him. I could not put my finger on it. I remember thinking, ever since he decided he wanted to be committed to the church, his commitment to our carefree and easy going marriage covenant was no more. If I knew then what I have become wise to now, I would have prayed day and night to cover my husband. As I look back, I now see that my husband had become committed to the church and not God. I knew he loved me but he wasn't patient with me like the Bible commanded him to be. He wanted to do good and he wanted to be seen as good. Unfortunately, I usually became an emotional target from the pressure of all the demands to look good, talk holy, and give freely, and say yes on demand to whatever the church asked of him.

It was an illusion of goodness. This went on for a few years. I discovered that there was a dark side of wanting to do good and be seen as a good person. I had always believed that kindness and selflessness were virtues to strive for, but little did I know that this desire could open the door for something far more insidious. That was spiritual abuse. As long as I was giving and fitting into the ideal box that others desired me to remain in, I believe they felt like they had a sense of control over me. I loved the Lord and I loved to teach the arts in ministry. However, it was as if my talents and intentions were being manipulated to serve someone else's agenda. But that's a tale for another day. It's one that still reminds me that we fight not against flesh and blood.

In the midst of this journey, I began to believe that my husband, too, had fallen into the trap of believing that doing good would guarantee that everything would fall into place. I felt he had convinced himself that as long as he continued to be a beacon of goodness, life would align itself perfectly in the kingdom.

However, this newfound belief started to conflict with our marriage. The very act of doing good for others began to overshadow our relationship. It became a thing of how much more good can we do from day to day. The genuine love and connection we once shared was slowly fading away, replaced by the pursuit of validation through acts of kindness. I must clarify, this was my point of view

.

It was during this turbulent time that we both learned a valuable lesson. We learned that doing a good thing is not always a God-directed thing. We had been so focused on external works and how it made us feel virtuous, that we had forgotten the true essence of spirituality. I knew this to be true because

I could do something amazing and turn right around and curse my husband verbally for making me angry.

God simply requires us to love and have faith. It's not about performing acts of kindness to gain approval from others. It's about embodying love and compassion in our everyday actions, without any other expectations.

As we reflected on our journey, we realized that true goodness comes from a place of authenticity and pure intentions. It doesn't seek validation or control; it simply seeks to spread love and make a positive impact.

With this newfound understanding, we embarked on a journey to rediscover the true meaning of goodness in our lives and our marriage. We let go of the need for external validation and focused on nurturing our connection and living a life guided by love and faith. Little by little, our relationship began to heal. We learned to prioritize each other and our shared values above any external expectations. Our acts of kindness are now genuine expressions of love, rather than a means to an end. And as we continued on this path, we discovered a deeper sense of fulfillment and joy. We realized that true goodness lies in the simplicity of love, and that by embodying this love, we can create a positive impact in our own lives and the lives of those around us.

This chapter of our lives taught us a valuable lesson - that the pursuit of goodness should never come at the expense of our relationships or our own well-being. It reminded us that true spirituality is not about following a set of rules or seeking validation, but about embodying love and faith in every aspect of our lives.

In any event my hubby's well doing opened some doors for more interaction with all different kinds of people and ministry. This too was also training for where God was intending to lead both of us. Although I almost never went along willingly, I still went. Most of the time I went begrudgingly and downright stubbornly. I know it was God that had a hand on my life because as I think back, I would secretly sulk about the company we had to entertain and the dark spirits that were dressed up in church clothes. I would always warn my husband concerning the dark spirits many of the so-called leaders were battling with. His response was always the same. Crystal! It's not our job to worry about that. As long as they don't touch my family, everything will be ok. My husband kept his promise. He assured me they would not harm us physically. I saw all the devilish spiritual attacks they launched against my family. I was so aggravated and weary during many seasons, that I wanted to resort back to physical fighting. At least, I would feel more satisfied in my flesh. I laugh to myself even now as I recount the thought. I would imagine myself just punching or kicking them one good time. Had I known what the enemy meant for evil, God would turn it around for my good. Had I only responded differently when the attacks came. Would I be further along in life? Was each incident a lesson or training for the warrior walk to present itself?

Chapter 6: THE BREAKING OF FORGIVENESS

Psalms 147:3 He heals the brokenhearted and binds up their wounds.

We were about 5 years into my husband accepting his call to ministry. I couldn't have been more angry, and untrusting of everyone. I would constantly warn him who was a hypocrite. He would constantly tell me to pray for them. I literally almost gave up. I made a plan. In my mind I had to protect myself before I had a spiritual death behind those walls that I was supposed to worship within. I planned to leave my husband when my children graduated from high school. I didn't want to disrupt their childhood and high school experience, so I stayed a few more years. As time progressed, I kept that plan in mind and nothing was changing it. I was so wrought in my spirit, I felt myself becoming bitter. At the same time, I joined a women's ministry outside of the church and I was getting stronger in my knowledge of warfare. I knew that two spirits couldn't live peaceably within me. I also knew I couldn't let down my guard. For I was convinced there were enemies all around me. I was awakened to another level as to who I was in the spirit by a Sista by the name of Besceglia. I grew spiritually and strong in the Lord. I enjoyed the ministry until a local young lady had persuaded the women in ways that were not pleasing to myself as a married woman and a growing warrior. It was a pivotal time in my life. I was waiting to leave my husband, and I made up my mind to leave the women's group I had joined. In the ordinary person's mind, I would appear to be in a lonely season, but that was far from true. God had me all the time. I felt invincible once again.

One night after photographing one of my largest weddings yet, my husband asked me to accompany him to Charlotte. I agreed to ride so he could drop off a car for his cousin. The ride up was peaceful. However, on the way back was something I could have never imagined in all my lifetime. The last thing I remember is my husband saying that he was going to get something to drink. He proceeded to turn into the store parking lot.

The next time I awoke I remember someone over me yelling hey! We're going to have to cut her out! I was groggy and couldn't feel a thing. The next thing that I remember is being on a cold table and someone speaking over me, saying, "we're going to have to put a hose in her side. Still groggy, I remember fighting and whoever was working on me needed several people to hold me down. I blanked back out for what seemed like days. The next time I awoke to my husband standing over my bed. My eyes opened slowly. I wiggled my toes and feet. I thought to myself, I think I was in an accident. I looked around the room and wiggled my toes again. Once I knew that I could wiggle my toes, I knew by the grace of God, I Could get back to where I was physically. It was a silent reassurance the Holy Spirit had given me. I quickly fell back to sleep.

Once my brother found I had awoken again, he came to my bedside. I was at peace and shared with him the vision I had while I was asleep. I told him that I saw our father. I described the vision and how the encounter took place. My brother leaned in as I described everything. I only told my brother Andre that dad said that I would be ok. I was more excited about telling my brother, I had seen our dad again more than anything. I was still in my hospital bed and the room was completely white. It was a peaceful atmosphere. In my vision, my father, who is now deceased, appeared by my bedside. He told me it was a very close call there for a while and they almost lost me. He continued on saying that I was out of the woods and now everything would be ok. I would believe what others say about visiting spirits not being true, but the confirmation of my encounter was confirmed a whole year later. My sister in law Ladawn told me what the doctors had said verbatim. A whole year had passed by since the accident. My sister in law Ladawn and my sister Cathea had revealed what the doctors had said about my injuries. The doctors told the family that it was touch and go and they almost lost me. The part they shared with me about my near-death experience was the same exact words my father shared with me in my dream. I never shared with anyone exactly what my father told me in my dream standing at my bedside. Therefore, I believe without a shadow of doubt that I had a true encounter and visitation. The next few people that entered my hospital room were key to my healing journey. I opened my eyes again and my Uncle Jeremiah was standing at the foot of my bed. He asked how I was feeling. I told him, I felt ok. I then asked him to pray one specific prayer for me. I asked that he pray that I would dance once more. I know beyond a shadow of doubt God answered that prayer. For the injuries I endured presented the tragedy of me possibly never walking again. The next visitor was a young prophetess by the name of Dejuan. She asked my husband if it was ok to anoint and pray over me. She poured the oil in her hand and walked to the other side of the room. When she walked back over to me, put her hand on my forehead. All I remember was her saying, "Father God". It seemed as though I blacked out for a few more days. The next time I awoke, I was out of ICU. The staff could not believe how much progress I was making in a short amount of time. The extent of my injuries were astounding. I cracked a bone at the base of my skull. My lungs collapsed twice, I bruised my aorta, my left pelvic fractures in three places, I had to get my mouth redone, and I fractured five of my ribs. I literally only stayed in the hospital for about two weeks. They sent me home after that. A home health nurse came to visit me at home. As he was kneeling on the floor filling out his paperwork while completing his assessments, he began to apologize. He said he didn't want to seem ignorant or rude. I already knew what he was leading up to. He too was astounded at the rate of my healing progress. I simply smiled and said, "yes sir". He informed me that after reviewing my chart and looking at me in the physical, things just didn't match up. He asked me if I was aware that I was a miracle. I looked down at him and again, I simply smiled. And replied," yes". I marveled at the fact that God would use this stranger to remind me that I had a bigger calling and my miracle had purpose. Although I was healing at a rapid speed, I had a long road ahead of me.

A few of the ladies from the church came to visit. They brought a donation and a few gifts. One of the most effective gifts I received was a book on forgiveness.

However, when I first saw the book, I turned my nose up at it. In my mind, I was thinking, I didn't need a book on forgiveness. Everybody else needed to ask for forgiveness. They were the ones who did me wrong. I set it to the side. It sat on the bench next to me for about two weeks. When all the calls and visits slacked up I had more time to ponder. My children went back to school and my husband couldn't stop working because He was our only source of income. I would have to sit in the same spot for 24 hours with help to use the restroom once or twice a day.

I was on five different medications to assist me with pain and keep me regular. I had nothing but time. I would glance at the book and roll my eyes. One day everyone was gone. Time got the best of me. I was so bored, I grabbed the book hoping to confirm what I expected. I expected that it was just another book that said forgive because God forgives. I wasn't trying to hear that or read it for that matter. Something supernatural happened when I opened the book and began to read. All of the anger, contention, and resentment surrounding what I thought the book to be about had disappeared. From the first page, I was drawn in. It was as if God was speaking Himself. I couldn't put the book down. I finished it in a matter of four days. I had so heard so many sermons and quotes, and other people's opinion on forgiveness, I had made my mind up that it was a bunch of words Christians would say to seem like they always did the right thing and their hearts were free of unforgiveness. It was as if God was working a work in my heart as I was reading the book. I literally felt like an entirely different person after finishing the book.

The day I finished reading the book, I was expecting a visit from the home health nurse. They were scheduled to come and assist because I still was unable to walk on my own. Today the nurse informed me that I would be taking a full shower for the first time. It had been an entire three or four months since I had been inside my shower. The nurse helped me inside the shower and onto the shower bench. I showered for the first time in a long time. The spirit directed me to look at the drain. I instantly heard the Holy Spirit say. "You are forgiven, and now that you fully understand forgiveness, I've washed all the bitterness, anger, and unforgiveness, down the drain. I stared down at the drain before getting out of the shower. I immediately felt a huge relief. It was as if one thousand burdens had been lifted off of my mind and spirit.

The next day, I was still at home alone during the day and I felt the strength to walk without the walker. I just knew I could and I did. I could feel the surge of power within my body that my hip and pelvic were healed in God speed. I certainly was not released to walk by any doctor. I had not even been released from the wheel chair yet. Secretly, I planned to walk before any man claimed I would be able to. That is exactly what I set my mind to do.

During the healing process I reviewed many things and relationships in my mind. I became more humble and able to control my temperament. The controlling of my temperament may have been partly because I couldn't walk yet but, I'm going to stand beside the fact that I was still controlling it for the time being. Although confined to a wheelchair for a couple months, I was still able to get around.

I remember one day my friend Camilla came when my husband was not home. She said, I'm kidnapping you. Let's go before your husband gets back. Her husband Steve had just purchased her a brand new BMW. She said I'm going to put this wheel chair in the trunk and we are going to go ride out. The crazy thing about it is that I was totally down. She gently rolled me down the ramp my husband had built in the garage in order to have wheelchair access. Camilla drove me to the ice cream shop. She told me not to worry about the car and go ahead and enjoy my ice cream in her brand new BMW. I will never forget it. We made it back home and she secured me back in the recliner before my husband came home. That was a beautiful, touching day. I needed that. I needed to see that good people still existed and the whole world wasn't against me.

God still had His hand on me guiding and molding me and softening my heart. For now I know a warrior needed to be only hard in opposition against the enemy. Leading a disciplined life for Christ was hard enough. I felt more comfortable not needing to be in war mode 24 hours a day and seven days a week. I came to the understanding that my heart needed to remain subtle and open for the move of the Holy Spirit. A warrior needed to know when to strike but they needed to also know when to protect. This strategy required balance. Gratefully, the afternoon I spent with Camilla had definitely opened the door for me to adhere to what the Holy Spirit was conditioning me for in the spirit. With this newfound spirit of balance, peace, and forgiveness, I began to reassess. I readjusted my mindset towards different things and my approach to different situations. I got around to communicating a spirit of forgiveness and actively carrying out forgiveness with individuals I had silent offenses with. Things began to shift for me in the spirit and in the physical. I completely severed relationships that were toxic and I began to embrace the plans the Father had strategically placed along my path in this life.

Chapter 7: ACCEPTING THE CHALLENGE TO FIGHT OR FLIGHT

Isaiah 58:6-7 to loose the chains of injustice and untie the cords of the yoke, set the oppressed free and break every yoke?

God presented the opportunity to co-found a new innovative women's ministry. Zeta Alpha Psi Sisterhood was founded on 1 Peter 2:9. We agreed that the ministry would be allocated as a sisterhood and not a sorority. I was already part of a sorority. Although sororities generally promote unity and community service, not every woman has the opportunity to meet requirements to become a member. We purposely went with the term sisterhood because in a sisterhood, all are invited whether they possessed a degree or not.   We the foundation that God was a requirement and God was our common denominator. However, it did not come without obstacles. We started with six prospects to build and by the time we entered our third year, four founders were still on the battlefield. Sharekia Reddick and her husband Darryl and myself and my husband Vincent.   The first five years presented battle after battle. As I look back again, I know for sure that we were definitely in warfare training. It appeared as if the enemy attempted to enter in every open door and crack possible and at every opportunity seen and unseen. We stood our ground against the enemy and refused to lose ground.   Today the sisterhood is a five-fold ministry which spans over more than six states with membership in India. We've become an international women's ministry. Now we understand the level of warfare that was presented. The intention of the enemy was to decimate us before we grew to fight the kingdom of darkness. As I continue to work within the Sisterhood, I learned first-hand how powerful and effective the warrior spirit is and how the years of training had not been so easy but very much needed.

Chapter 8: ASSURED VICTORY IN BATTLE

---

2 Chronicles 20:17   You will not need to fight this battle. Stand firm, hold your position, and see the salvation of the Lord on your behalf, O Judah and Jerusalem.' Do not be afraid and do not be dismayed. Tomorrow go out against them, and the Lord will be with you."

It appears that the enemy may have won some battles but he clearly can never win the war. Warriors are specifically trained in all aspects of spiritual warfare time and time and time again. God declares that the battle is already won and the victory is already ours in   Deuteronomy 20:4 For the Lord your god is One who goes with you to fight for you against your enemies to give you victory.

In Fact there is a divine victory. This happens when God fights for us. This type of victory happens when the victory comes beyond a shadow of a doubt from God alone. There were many times when I didn't even have to fight. It was during those times when God proved to be my battle ax and shield.

I had reached a season in my life where fear was no longer my portion. I had adopted the notion that fear was really an acronym with a hidden meaning of false evidence appearing real. Fear presents fake news and our imagination advertises it and publicizes it to be a greater threat than it really is. I wish I had known that in my adolescent years. I now realize that as a child I had let my imagination run wild. I imagined all types of wild monsters were in the dark.

Although I never saw one, in my mind I believed they existed. For that one reason, fear continuously gripped me every night the lights went out. Now that I'm older and strapped with the Word of God, I now know better. The enemy is a master of deception and can present things to you that only seem real. The enemy is the father of lies. Tactics used are sprinkled with a little truth or past trauma only to make it appear believable. Many times we fall for this level of deception because of the small part of truth that is attached to the lie.

However, we are to keep in mind that nothing evil, dark, or negative in our imagination, mind, and spirit will come from the Lord Almighty. Therefore, negativity, darkness, and doubts must come from the enemy. The Lord addresses our imaginations in 2 Corinthians 10:5-6. Scripture reads, "Casting down imaginations and every high thought that exalts itself against the Kingdom of God, and bringing into captivity every thought to the obedience of Christ." This simply means if it doesn't line up with the Word of God, it must be brought down and casted, out. The Word of God says to think on these good things. Philippians 4:8 KJV : Finally, brethren, whatsoever things are true, whatsoever things are honest, whatsoever things are just, whatsoever things are pure, whatsoever things are lovely, whatsoever things are of good report; if there be any virtue, and if there be any praise, think on these things.

God is good and the enemy is and will always be evil. Therefore, you will know that if you have an evil thought or image in your mind, it is coming from the enemy. We are reminded to keep our minds steadfast on the Lord.

Again, If I only knew this as a child. Because I didn't know who I was in the spirit, I operated as the enemy whispered in my ear. The enemy always whispered wick thoughts to my imagination. It kept me afraid of what people thought of me. My retaliation was to fight. In my mind, if they were afraid of me then they would not bother me. Unfortunately, they did not know just how afraid I was to unleash what I imagined was inside of me. I knew and felt that it was something powerful. For some reason the enemy had me to believe that that type of power was a bad thing. But now I am reminded of 2 Timothy 1:7 - For God hath not given us the spirit of fear; but of POWER, and of love, and of a sound mind. Isn't that just like the enemy? He is constantly on the prowl to make bad seem good and good appear to be something bad.

If we don't know the truth, fear keeps an unhealthy grip on us. If we aren't careful, we allow the enemy access to run rampant in our life, imagination, relationships, and dreams. We could inadvertently open the door for the spirit of fear just by believing or coming into agreement with the enemy whispers. We must understand that parts of our bodies possess the gates to our soul. Our ears are a gateway to hearing. I could have allowed the spirit of fear by succumbing to it when hearing my siblings scream there was a boogie man. Our eyes are also a gateway. We could own fear by watching scary movies and believing them. Our mind is also a powerful gateway. We could also own fear by constantly replaying in our minds the lies of the enemy.

Fortunately, I became grounded in the Word and had grown into a spiritual warrior. The victory didn't come overnight. As with any good thing, it took work.

The road to victory came after I had enough of the enemy beating up on me, keeping me in bondage, and holding me back from the mandate placed on my life. I asked the Father one question that would change my whole life.

I thought back on when I cried out for God to show me great things? My soul needed better reasons than just existing, going to work, going to church, and home. I needed more. That day I know God heard my plea. Over the next few years, I began to not only study but experience deep warfare. I used the bold fight I had inside of me to battle for the Lord. It was a tedious journey. I made many mistakes and was often misunderstood. My strong passion to protect God's people was often mistaken for anger.

Chapter 9: WINNING THE BATTLE

"For our struggle is not against flesh and blood, but against the rulers, against the authorities, against the powers of this dark world and against the spiritual forces of evil in the heavenly realms. Therefore, put on the full armor of God, so that when the day of evil comes, you may be able to stand your ground, and after you have done everything, to stand." Ephesians 6:12-13:

By this time, I'd experienced enough of the enemy. I had allowed the enemy to make me shut down and or fight in the wrong manner long enough. After co-founding the sisterhood ministry I experienced more opportunities to fight the godly way. It turned out that standing in the gap as one of God's Spiritual Warriors has always been one of my mandates. In this season, not only would I get to fight, which my flesh loves to do anyway; I would no longer run and take flight. I now stand strong and send the enemy to flight. I'm using the same boldness I allowed the enemy to abuse me with. Now I fight God's way. I'm now fighting with a sword so sharp, it kills all foolishness the enemy brings my way. Hebrews 4:12 says, "For the Word of God is alive and active. Sharper than any double-edged sword, it penetrates even to divide soul and spirit, joints and marrow; it judges the thoughts and attitudes of the heart." The Word of God is the ultimate truth. We can find boldness and safety in knowing it is our greatest weapon. We must be reminded that our battles are not against physical enemies, but against spiritual forces that are beyond a natural existence. It encourages us to put on the full armor of God, which is Founded most heavily on TRUTH. Knowing the truth of our power and strength gives us a favored advantage over the enemy.   By relying on God's truth and God's strength, and equipping ourselves with His armor, we can stand firm to win the battle every time.

I've traveled from a place of physical fight to one of spiritual fortitude. As a child, I sometimes have acted out in ways that hurt others, but through self-reflection and spiritual growth, I've transformed into a warrior of the spirit. My armor is now empathy, compassion, and understanding, and my sword is the wisdom of my power in the Lord. I've gained valuable spiritual knowledge along the way. I've also learned to wield my experiences, both the triumphs and the struggles, as tools to uplift, inspire, and enlighten others. My transformation is a testament to the power of personal growth and the spiritual capacity for redemption.

Today, I stand boldly with my sword. I don't always get it right on the first swing. Sometimes I mistaken my soldiers in the ministry as foes. This happens because I'm still a work in progress and sometimes I have to remind myself to bring the walls down and work only in the strength of the Lord and not my own. I also am reminded to get out of the way of myself to avoid self-infliction. That means to fight as a warrior, I need to lean not towards my own understanding and trust God's Word of guaranteed victory. Through each new obstacle and revelation I shall continue to call for backup from the one and only true and Living God. A worldwide undefeated tag team champion. For when I am uncertain, He shall provide a peace that surpasses all understanding. When I am tired, I know He will never fail me in the battle. When others would fall away, or grow weary, I know He will remain and never forsake me. With God on my side, a pure heart, and yielding my sharp sword which is the unfaltering Word of God, the victory is mine every time. Selah!

About Author

Crystal Smith is an accomplished photographer of Smith Photography; an innovative photography company which also uses their gifts and talents to pour back into the community. Crystal was born the youngest of five children. She is the daughter of Margaret Crosby, and the late Lee Williams. She graduated from Glasgow High School in Newark, Delaware. While matriculating at Glasgow High, she actively participated in cheerleading, basketball, and track. After graduating, she attended Allen University where She competed in public speaking on tri- state level, winning several awards. She was inducted into Sigma Tau Delta English Honors Society in 1993 by her English professor Dr. Sandra Black. She remained very active during her 4 years at Allen University. She served four years as captain of the cheering squad, and took up dance under the late Harold Odom, a former dance instructor at Benedict College. She pledged Mu Chapter of Alpha Kappa Alpha Sorority Inc. After graduating in 1994 with a Bachelor of Arts in English; she accepted a position at Spike Boykin Studios. While working, she honed her photography skills. She married in 1997 to Vincent Smith.

They have two children Vincent II and Alecia Smith. In 1997 Smith founded her own dance group, "Umoja"; . She has taught dance for over 20 years with clients such as the after school youth under contract for the United States Army of Fort Jackson Army Base and statewide for school age youth. Her credentials include the South Carolina Commission of Artists in Residency. She now works with various youth dance organizations in South Carolina. She is one of the founders of Zeta Alpha Psi Sisterhood. Their purpose is to empower women and youth world-wide.

Together her and her husband Vincent Smith have founded the ministry Favor of Grace which empowers and equips God's people through the Word of God, in different communities and internationally.

For the weapons of
our warfare are not
carnal, but mighty
through God to the
pulling down of
strong holds.